Written by Gail Blasser Riley

STECK-VAUGHN
ELEMENTARY · SECONDARY · ADULT · LIBRARY

A Harcourt Classroom Education Company

www.steck-vaughn.com

CONTENTS

Chapter 1

Picture Writing and Special Signs

Have you ever wanted to tell a friend something secret? Maybe you whispered. Maybe you wrote a note to **communicate** your idea. Maybe you used a special wave or other hand sign to send your message.

People have communicated for thousands of years by speaking, by writing, and by making signs. When people first came together to live and work, they used sounds and gestures, or body movements, to get their ideas across. Some gestures became hand signs. The sounds gradually became spoken languages. As time went on, some people invented ways to write down their language.

One of the oldest kinds of writing is called **cuneiform** (kyoo NEE uh fohrm). Cuneiform writing wasn't like our writing today. It didn't have letters that formed words. Instead, it had **pictographs**, or pictures. Each pictograph stood for an object, idea, or syllable. For example, a drawing of a foot meant "go." Few people knew how to write in cuneiform. The people that did were called **scribes**.

Cuneiform is easy to recognize. Its pictographs have wedge-shaped lines. To make these lines, a scribe needed a stylus. A stylus was a sticklike tool. Some styluses were made of plants called reeds. Some were made of bone or metal. Using the stylus, scribes carved pictographs into wet clay tablets.

At first, cuneiform pictographs were written one under another, in columns. A scribe would start at the left on one side of the tablet. When he had filled that side, he would turn the tablet over. The scribe would then start at the right. In later cuneiform, the pictographs were written across, from left to right.

Look at the cuneiform pictographs at left below. Pretend you are a scribe, and your pencil is a stylus. Then use the pictographs to carve a sentence in a flat piece of clay. Add your own pictographs, too. Try writing your pictographs in columns.

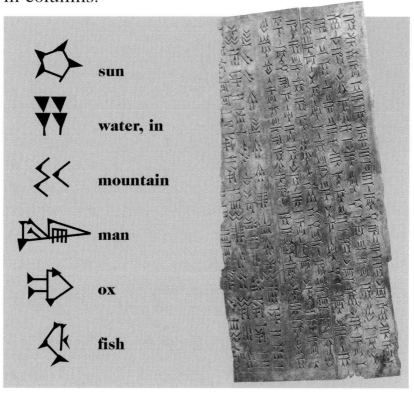

sun

water, in

mountain

man

ox

fish

A cuneiform tablet from about 500 B.C.

Hieroglyphics (hi ruh GLIF icks) was another kind of pictograph writing. It was created by the ancient Egyptians. The word *hieroglyphic* means "sacred carving."

Hieroglyphic writing was mainly used to record important ideas and events. It was often carved into stone temples and monuments. Hieroglyphic writing was more **complicated** than cuneiform writing. Hieroglyphs usually stood for sounds or groups of sounds, not objects or ideas.

Sometimes hieroglyphs were written from top to bottom in columns. Sometimes they were written across in rows. The writing usually moved from right to left. That's just the opposite of the way people write in English.

After a while new kinds of writing took the place of hieroglyphics. Thousands of years passed. No one remembered how to write hieroglyphs or even what they meant. Then in 1799 a man in Egypt discovered a thick stone tablet with hieroglyphic writing on it. It was named the Rosetta Stone after the town where it was found.

The inscription on the stone reads:

THE ROSETTA STONE

**The Rosetta Stone has the same message in three
different languages.**

For 20 years people tried to figure out the
ancient writing. Finally a teacher in France figured
out how hieroglyphics worked. He was able to
read the Rosetta Stone. The writing on the stone
tells about the crowning of an Egyptian king.

In 1812 a young boy in France was playing with the tools in his father's shop. The boy accidentally cut one of his eyes. He soon became blind in both eyes. He could not go to the same schools that other children attended. He studied hard at a special school in Paris, but he could not read books.

The boy's name was Louis Braille. For years he tried to create a way to read by touch. At last he began working with raised dots and dashes on cardboard. This kind of writing was called point writing. It had once been used to send army messages in code.

Braille completed his writing system in 1829. Today people who cannot see can read books written in **Braille**. They can even write Braille with a special typewriter.

You can find Braille next to the "up" and "down" buttons outside elevator doors. It is also next to the floor numbers inside the elevator. People who cannot see feel the raised dots on the buttons. They read the information with their fingers.

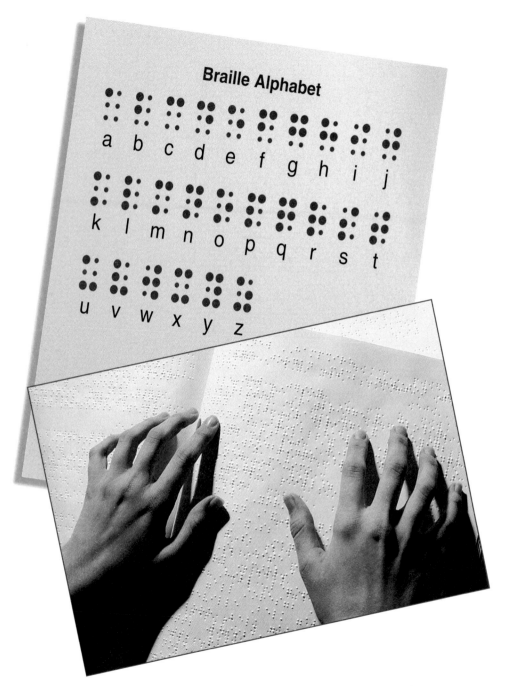

Braille opened up the world of books to people who cannot see.

9

Shorthand

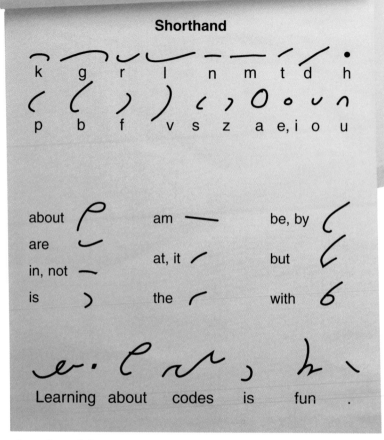

Shorthand has simple marks for letters and words.

Shorthand is another special kind of writing. When people use shorthand, they write simple marks to stand for letters, single words, and groups of words. Shorthand is a very fast way of writing. Business people, newspaper reporters, and court reporters have used shorthand for years. These people must be able to write very quickly.

Today's court reporters use special machines to record everything said during a trial. All the keys on these machines can be pushed at once. Machine shorthand can record more than 200 words per minute. Modern news reporters and business people often rely on tape recorders and computers. But some people still use shorthand when they want to write quickly.

A court-reporting machine

There are lots of special ways of writing. What about special ways of speaking? When you talk to your friends, you use spoken language, and your friends hear what you are saying. What if you want to talk to someone who cannot hear?

This is what happened to a Frenchman, Charles Michel de l'Épée (lay PAY), in the 1700s. He visited a family with two daughters who could not hear. The girls tried very hard to communicate. They nodded, used gestures, and made expressions with their faces. But l'Épée couldn't understand everything they wanted to tell him.

l'Épée decided to invent a language for people who could not hear. Because he saw deaf people communicating with their body, l'Épée created a language that used a different position of the fingers for each letter of the alphabet.

Later, signs that stood for complete words were developed. Then people could use a system of finger and arm movements to communicate quickly. Now many people all around the world who cannot hear use sign language. They talk to each other, and they talk to people who can hear.

Sign Language Alphabet

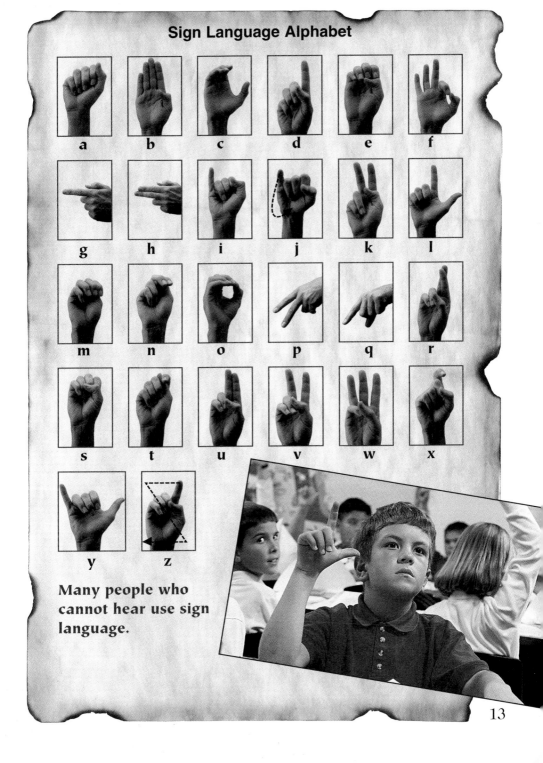

Many people who cannot hear use sign language.

Before radios were invented, sailors needed to send messages. How did they do that? They used **semaphore**. Semaphore was a flag alphabet. Sailors held the flags in different places to stand for the letters of the alphabet. For example, one flag straight up and the other to the side stood for the letter *p*. With semaphore, sailors could send messages to other ships and to people on the shore.

Semaphore worked only during the day. How did sailors and others communicate in the dark? One way was to use flashes of light. Each flash— long, short, high, low—had a meaning. Sailors, train workers, and airline pilots still use light **signals** to send messages at night.

Would you like to find out more about special ways to communicate? Maybe you'd like to send secret messages to friends. Read on!

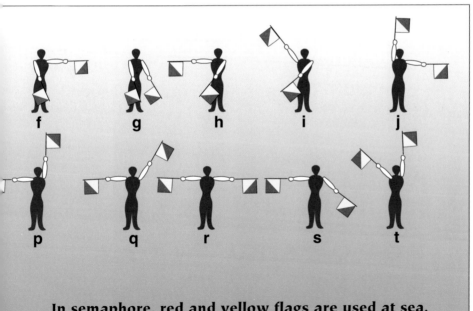

In semaphore, red and yellow flags are used at sea. Red and white flags are used on land.

CHAPTER 2

Ciphers

Let's say you need a fast, easy way to write a message to a friend. Suppose you don't want anyone else to be able to read it. You might use a **cipher** (SY phur). A cipher is a secret way of writing.

To use a cipher, you replace the letters in your message with different letters. Take a look at the **cipher key** below. It is for a substitution cipher, because one letter is replaced with another. The substitution cipher is the most popular kind of cipher.

A	B	C	D	E	F	G	H	I	J	K	L	M
B	C	D	E	F	G	H	I	J	K	L	M	N

N	O	P	Q	R	S	T	U	V	W	X	Y	Z
O	P	Q	R	S	T	U	V	W	X	Y	Z	A

To write a message with this cipher, you change every letter in your message to the letter below it. Everywhere you need an *A*, write a *B*. Everywhere you need a *B*, write a *C*, and so on. Each letter in your message appears as the letter after it in the alphabet.

Let's say you want to send the following message:

MEET ME AT THE GYM AFTER SCHOOL.

When you turn your message into a cipher, you **encode** the message. It will then look like this:

NFFU NF BU UIF HZN BGUFS TDIPPM.

When your friend takes the message out of the cipher, your friend **decodes** the message.

Now try the cipher key below to write the same message. This cipher key is for another kind of cipher. In it, letters are replaced with numbers.

A	B	C	D	E	F	G	H	I	J	K	L	M
1	2	3	4	5	6	7	8	9	10	11	12	13

N	O	P	Q	R	S	T	U	V	W	X	Y	Z
14	15	16	17	18	19	20	21	22	23	24	25	26

You and your friends can make up your own substitution ciphers by replacing letters with numbers or other letters. As long as the person sending the cipher and the person receiving it have the key, the cipher will be easy to decode.

You may want to try another popular cipher. In it, letters within words are mixed up. Here is the message from page 17. Look at how the letters in each word have been mixed up.

TEME EM TA ETH MYG FERAT OOHCLS.

Ciphers like the ones you've just used have been popular throughout history. In the 1560s, Mary, Queen of Scots, created and used her very own cipher.

Mary tried to take over England. The English queen, Elizabeth I, put Mary in jail. Even in jail, Mary communicated with her followers in Scotland, but she had to make sure no one else could read her messages. Her cipher is well known today. Try writing your name and a short message in this famous cipher.

Mary, Queen of Scots, and her cipher key

Ciphers were used centuries ago. They're still used today. Have you ever seen price tags that made no sense? Maybe you've seen them in a sports card shop or a store where used clothing is sold.

Ciphers on price tags tell the amount the seller paid. For example, *CQMN* marked on a sports card could be a cipher for $12.50. The *C* could mean "1." The *Q* could mean "2." The *M* could mean "5," and the *N* could mean "0."

The seller has the key to the cipher. She could look at the tag and decide how much more to ask for the sports card. But you would not know how much the card cost her.

The letters in the top tag are a cipher for $15.50. Can you figure out the price on the bottom tag? The answer is on page 40.

Thomas Jefferson and his cipher wheel

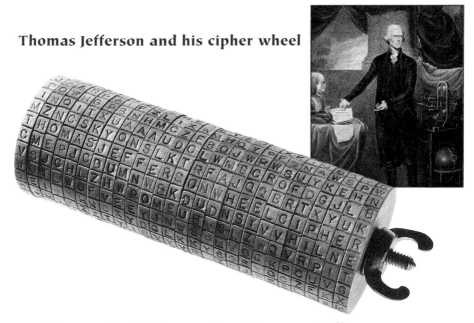

You probably know that Thomas Jefferson was a President of the United States. Did you know that he often used ciphers to communicate with his friends? He also invented the cipher wheel.

The cipher wheel was made of 36 thin wooden wheel disks. Each disk could spin. On the rim of the disks, Jefferson carved the letters of the alphabet in mixed-up order. He made another cipher wheel exactly like the first. He could then send messages to whoever had the second cipher wheel. That person simply matched the first row of letters and figured out the rest of the message.

CHAPTER 3

Codes

Ciphers and **codes** are very much alike, but they have one main difference. Ciphers substitute one letter (or sometimes one number) for another letter. Codes are more complicated. In a code, a single word, number, or letter replaces whole words or groups of words—or groups of numbers. In other words, for the word *friend*, a cipher might change the *f* to *g*, the *r* to *s*, and so on. But a code changes the whole word. For example, the number *100* might stand for *friend*. Or *ship* might stand for *friend*.

Long before telephones, telegraph lines ran across the land. They allowed people to send electronic "beeps" over long distances. In 1838

Morse code keys—old and new

Samuel Morse invented a beep code for the letters of the alphabet. He also invented a special kind of machine called a key to send **Morse code** messages over telegraph lines.

Morse code messages are sent by a person tapping on the key. Each time the key is tapped, it sends a high-pitched sound. A quick tap on the key makes a short sound. It is called a dit. A slower tap on the key makes a longer sound. It is called a dah. When Morse code is written, a dot (•) stands for a dit. A dash (—) stands for a dah. Morse code is one of the most famous codes. It has been widely used on boats and ships.

In Morse code, letters of the alphabet are sent by tapping groups of dits and dahs. Look at the Morse code alphabet to see how you would send an S O S, a call for help.

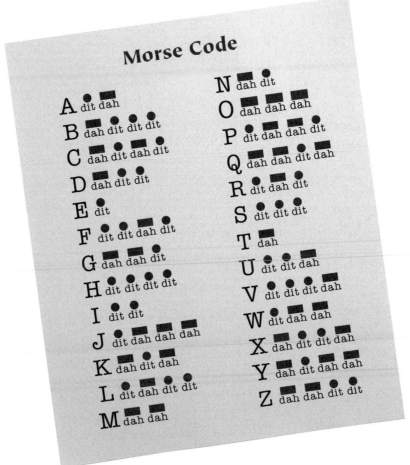

Written Morse code is made of dots and dashes that stand for sounds.

You may not use Morse code in everyday life, but many codes are used every day. Next time you go to the grocery store, look at the code the checker scans to get the price of each item. You'll see a series of lines with numbers below them. You might hear a checker call these the "bar code." It's really a Universal Product Code (UPC).

The UPC has been used since 1973. It contains important information. For example, it might tell whether the item is meat, cheese, or poultry. It might tell whether the item is a health product. Or it might tell whether the item is sold only in a special store. The UPC information is sent to the main computer in the store.

The UPC is used on many different products.

Another code that computers understand is the ZIP code. The ZIP code is part of an address. It is written just after the abbreviation for the state. Every location in the United States has a ZIP code. The code helps the post office send each letter to the right person.

Special computers look at the front of each letter and read the ZIP code. The first numeral of the code tells the post office what part of the country the letter is going to. The next numerals stand for more information, such as the part of a state or city where the address is.

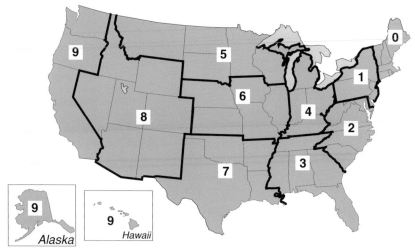

The numerals on this map are the first ones in ZIP codes. Which numeral does your ZIP code start with?

ATMs make use of codes. The codes help banks to keep people's money safe.

Have you ever gone with someone to get money from a cash machine, or automated teller machine (ATM)? First the ATM reads the number on the card. That number is a code for the person's bank account. Then the person enters a personal identification number (PIN). The PIN is also a code. It tells the computer that it's okay to give the person the money.

Ciphers and codes can do a very good job of keeping secrets. Would you like to learn a few secrets of your own to help you break codes and ciphers? Turn the page!

CHAPTER 4

Breaking Ciphers and Codes

Code-breakers are people who work to figure out ciphers and codes. First they may think about the reason for the cipher or code. For example, a cipher might be used during a war. If it is, it may be a top-secret war message. The code-breakers would think about words often used during war.

Another way to break codes and ciphers is to look for frequently used numbers, letters, or symbols. If the cipher contains many *X*'s, the letter *X* may stand for a letter often used in English, such as *I* or *A*.

Breaking a code can be very hard. Code-breakers often spend hours, days, or even years trying to guess the key that will unlock the code. During World War I and World War II, famous code-breakers spent years figuring out the keys to enemy codes.

Which do you think is easier—encoding or decoding? Most people think it's much easier to encode. After all, when you encode, you're the one making up the code or the cipher. Trying to figure out what a cipher or code means can be much harder.

Do you think you can decode a cipher message? Try this one:

R ZN TLRMT GL GSV NLERVH NVVG NV ZG GSV WLLI RU BLF DZMG GL XLNV.

Before you begin, read the tips on pages 30–31.

Tips for Breaking Ciphers and Codes

☑ Copy the message onto a new sheet of paper. Have a pencil and eraser handy. Be sure to leave space to write below each letter. Be prepared to erase letters that don't work and to try new letters.

☑ A letter that stands alone in the encoded message is probably *I* or *A*. So write *I* or *A*—or both—below each letter that stands alone in your message.

☑ The nine letters used most often in messages are *E, T, A, O, N, R, D, S,* and *H*. Look through the secret message carefully. Which letter is used most often? First, try *E*. If that doesn't work, try *T*, and so on.

☑ If you see a group of three letters, try *THE* to see if this letter combination will work.

☑ When you see a word with two letters, try *ON, IN, OF, IS, AN,* and *AM*. There's a good chance one of these will work.

☑ When you see two of the same letter side-by-side, try *OO, EE, SS, LL,* and *TT*. These are common combinations.

☑ Words sometimes end in *S, ED,* or *ING*, so try these word endings to see if they work.

☑ You should find at least one vowel in each word.

☑ Take your time decoding the message. Remember to use trial and error.

Now look at the message again and try to decode it. When you're done, turn to page 40 to find the decoded message.

R ZN TLRMT GL GSV NLERVH
NVVG NV ZG GSV WLLI RU BLF
DZMG GL XLNV.

CHAPTER 5

Hidden Messages and Cipher Machines

You've been reading about ways to create and break ciphers and codes. But there are ways to make your messages even harder—maybe impossible—to read!

One way is to hide the message. People have hidden messages inside secret parts of jewelry boxes, clocks, suitcases—just about any place you can think of.

One of the most famous examples of a hidden message is from long ago. A king shaved a man's head. He tattooed a secret message on the man's head and waited for the man's hair to grow back. Then he sent the man to another leader with the message "Shave my head." After the man's head was shaved, the other leader could read the message!

You can send hidden messages, too. You don't need a secret hiding place, and you don't need to shave anyone's head. Your hidden message will be impossible for people to read unless they know about invisible ink. Invisible ink has been used for hundreds of years. In the United States, George Washington and spies used invisible ink to send messages.

Colorless fruit juices and milk can be used as invisible ink. These inks "appear" when a light bulb or hair dryer is used to heat them. Pairs of

Salt water can be used to make invisible ink.

chemicals are used as invisible ink, too. One chemical is used to write the message. The other is used to make the writing show. To send messages in invisible ink, use the directions that follow.

Invisible Ink Messages

Gather these things:
- 2 small glasses
- a tablespoon
- 3 tablespoons of water
- 2 tablespoons of table salt
- smooth white paper
- an artist's paintbrush or a cotton swab
- a pencil

■ Put the salt and water in a glass and stir the mixture. Let it sit for about half an hour. Some of the salt will settle at the bottom of the glass. Pour the salt water above it into the other glass.

■ The salt water is your invisible ink. Dip the paintbrush or cotton swab into the salt water and write your message on the paper. Then let the ink dry.

■ To see your invisible message, rub the side of a pencil lead over the paper. Presto! Your message will appear.

E-mail messages are not private.

Sometimes you may think that what you write is private. You might think the e-mail messages you send on a computer are private. They are not. Other people can read your e-mail. Many companies are looking for new ways to make e-mail secret.

The computer is not the first machine to turn messages into ciphers or codes. During World War I, special machines were invented to type out messages in cipher. These machines looked like typewriters, but they had two keyboards. One was used to type the plain message. The second keyboard changed the message into cipher.

Ciphers, codes, and hidden messages have been used for centuries to send important information. But they can be fun, as well. Try your hand at making a cipher machine. Just follow the directions.

How to Make a Cipher Machine

- Find a soda can or any other cylinder.

- Cut two thin strips of white paper, each long enough to fit around the can.

- On the first strip, write the alphabet in order. On the second strip, write the alphabet in any mixed-up order. Make sure the letters are spaced exactly the same on both strips.

- Tape each strip together end-to-end around the can. Make sure the strip with the normal alphabet is above the other strip.

- Choose a letter on each strip and line up the two letters. These two letters are your key letters.

Now you're ready to start encoding your message. Remember: if you want a friend to figure out the message, you'll need to give your friend the key letters and your cipher machine!

Glossary

Braille a system for reading by touch

cipher letters or numbers that replace letters in a message

cipher key the clue to how to solve a cipher

code words, numbers, or signs that replace other words

communicate to send and receive messages

complicated detailed

cuneiform a kind of writing that uses pictures

decode to figure out what a cipher or code message means

encode to turn a message into a cipher or a code

hieroglyphics a kind of writing that uses pictures

Morse code a kind of code in which dots and dashes stand for letters of the alphabet

pictograph a picture that stands for an object, idea, or syllable

scribe someone who writes

semaphore a way to communicate with flags

shorthand a fast way of writing with marks that stand for letters.

signal a sign or picture

Index

Answer to tag cipher on page 20: $27.00

Answer to secret message on page 32: I am going to the movies. Meet me by the door if you want to come.

Note: The front cover contains the word *codes* written in five different codes and ciphers.